Insignificant Time Capsule © 2023 Kirby Peterson



Presentation by *BookLeaf Publishing*

Web: www.bookleafpub.com

E-mail: info@bookleafpub.com

ISBN: 9789358738056

First edition 2023

# Insignificant Time Capsule

## Kirby Peterson

BookLeaf Publishing

India | USA | UK

*Thank you to everyone who has encouraged me
to keep writing, keep creating, and keep
exploring paths that lead me to myself.*

# ACKNOWLEDGEMENT

I am grateful for the time that I spent with my travelling companions during the summer of 2023 at Warm Heart in Mexico City. Additionally, my time spent volunteering with Pozo de Vida was a great experience, and I appreciate the staff's willingness to share a bit of their lives with me.

# PREFACE

This short collection of poems was written in the summer of 2023 in both Mexico City, Mexico and Denver, Colorado, USA. Many of poems are closer to the beginning of the rough draft spectrum than I might prefer or have been somewhat rushed to publication, but sometimes the writing process is like that. Some themes include personal relationships, late night ruminations, and personal/philosophical ideas.

 This compilation is a brief glimpse into my mind during a specific period of my life. The time wasn't anything particularly special in and of itself but, as with a lot of writing, it can serve as a bit of a personal time capsule.

 I hope at least something within the following pages resonates with you. Perhaps it will inspire you to write your own. Maybe it will give voice to something you've been trying to say. However it finds you, now that it is out in the world, everything else is just interpretation.

# el Shabbat de Compas

Something like family
 A community of one mind
 Let's share bread together.

Let's make it a ritual
A tradition worth continuing
Put away your devices
Leave behind all your vices.

Stop.
Don't even bury your dead
The roots will take hold
They'll reach for your heartstrings
And pull you down where
Not even Death sings.

Delight.
See what is around you
All the faces teaming with life
The flora breathing for you
And the fauna alongside
All are your sister
Each cell was you
Or will be you.

Worship.
Adore the beauty all around you.
Recognize the majesty inside, around,
And above you
You are not your own
You're not alone
Your breath is precious.

Yah…weh…
Yah…weh…
Yah…weh…

A custom worth repeating
A rite worth practicing
A ritual worth embracing.

Inhale and the world breathes
With you.

Yah…weh…
Yah…weh…
Yah…weh…

Exhale and your uncertainties
Fade into dust.

Yah…weh…
Yah…weh…
Yah…weh…

If only for a moment
It's only a moment
But oh what a moment
A precious, fleeting moment.

# (Still) Mercy

"Where were You?"

stumbling door to door.

you were too preoccupied,
too engrossed in their platform,
too transfixed on your agenda.

"Why didn't You tell me?"

My words passed through you.
you could hear, but rarely listened.
My tears didn't fit into your
sanded down, smooth, and sanitized +.

"i thought i knew You."

you painted over Me
with your comfort.
you replaced Me
with who you thought–
how you thought–
I Am.

"But You promised us."

and My promises remain.
unconditional means
there are no conditions,
no prerequisites,
no expectations.

# Today I am the Inquisitor

Living on the other side of yesterday
 may not be a simple task
 but it's our exclusive option.

Every present moment
fades quickly into past
without so much as a lament.

Everything is new,
even the dust
drained from stars,
collecting in jars.

Words repeated,
jumbled, and recollected
flash and fade.

We all spark
for an instant
denying the
swimming smoke,
as if our
agnosticism creates reality
as bills lead to laws.

Denial is refusal.
It is self-deception.
Denial will not
hold our ashes
forever distant
from our grasp.

Every second passes
never to be outdone
by the first.

Now everything
is new. Tomorrow everything
is empty. Yesterday everything
was.

Still, paradoxically
time is a gear,
a cog transfixed
to countless others.

Swimming in this sea
we see only through water,
our consciousnesses
the ever-present filter.

Will we ever
discover what lies
beyond our understanding,

just past our shelter?

Is there an edge
to who we are,
to where we can be,
between life
and the stars?

# The Restless Revolution

What don't we know
with so many years,
so many lives,
so long ago?

We've lost so much
to arrive at this moment,
but all the "what if's"
seem futile to the present.

Maybe fickle or futile
to some, but think of
the forgotten.

Consider the
children born
into slavery
who never knew
a day of freedom.

Or what about the
men who ripped
their very own freedom
in a momentary
lapse of judgment?

And still the women
who were burned
at the stake,
falsely accused
and condemned
to an early end.

All the innocent.
All the people
sleeping in cells
still fighting
the good fight.

How do any
of us sleep so
soundly?

If one of us
is encaged
we're not
truly free.

These musings
overwhelm me,
but how much more
painful they must be
to the innocent,
the ones left behind,
the fighters still

fighting.

Those at the top
claim "resistance
is futile," but that is
the true propaganda.

Resistance is power.
Narrative is the tool.
Education is the toolbox.
Collaboration is the key.

There is such a
greater space
in between every
overlapping oval
and confining,
coinciding,
and colliding
quadrilateral
than they've
attempted to insert
into our interiors.

Your difference unites
me to you. My flame
ignites you to me.
We are one
and we are many.

# Dreams at Bay without a Ship to Sail

Eyelids quickly drooping,
 gravity pulling me down.

How common are these words?
How mundane their flow
into your ears!

Drifting slowly
but falling quickly.

Nothing previously
unspoken, nothing
new under the sun.

Why are you
still reading?
Why am I
not sleeping?

As I lay me
in your dreams,
the sandman sews
my eyes behind
their seams.

I'm awake but
sleep talking, estranged
from my dreams. The
playful chatter
to my right and
in front of me
detracts me-
it distracts me.

A steady rhythm,
is it a heartbeat,
the rhythmic drum,
or the gentle hum
of white noise
between
 varied
 states
 of
 consciousness?

# From the shoulders of a thousand giants

Gilded empires emblazoned
with the sweat of
the proletariat, soaked
in the blood of
the expendable.

The high and mighty
now blind our eyes
and deafen our ears
with diversion,
recreation, and
leisure.

Get down from
your high horse
and stand on
the front lines.
Come quickly
to the shore,
the water's warm,
the oysters are fresh.

This world is yours
after all, we're just

living in it, living too
on borrowed time.

See our backs:
never straight, but
when we stand at
attention. The
glistening you covet
is not gold, but sweat
from our brow.

You'll never be the
Common Man.
You'll never be our
Every Man.

Though you may
try to fool us swiftly
we see beyond
your thin disguise.
You're not
the only jester
in this courtyard.

Our senses behold
what you don't tell us.
We know what lies
beneath your fold.

Your very own
paranoia cripples
you. You send your
hired hands
into the dark
to peer into
our clandestine
meetings,
all the while
your heel
exposed. You'll
be soon dethroned.

# Love, Hope, and Potential

A featherless pillow, a fatherless orphan,
no one to respond to the endless ringing.
"Dead men tell no tales," they say, but
misplaced dreams only produce tragic stories.

Abandoned hopes, unfulfilled potential,
unrequited
love, they follow the dead end road to despair.
Hope unfulfilled is no hope at all.
Potential wasted is the final wisp of smoke from
an extinguished candle.
One-sided infatuation is just that; it is
not love, despite the convincing and
enticing tongue with which she speaks.

Run far, run fast from Romance young one,
She will not satisfy you. She will only leave
you wanting more. She'll welcome you
aboard, but run aground on a shallow
sandbar. Do not get caught
in her clutches before her grip is too
tight to release you.

Please heed my advice, don't let
her become your vice. Remove

yourself from her grasp, leave
before you can never look back.

Seek out true hope.
Find real love.
Do not abandon your dreams
out of fear.

Swim to shore if you must, but
do not become complacent in the
status quo. There are too many
of us floating with the current,
we don't need one more.

And if it is your dream to
rescue those who cannot
swim, forget not your own
life jacket. Firmly affix your
mask before reaching for others'.

# Vacant, Meaningless Words

Connected, dissected, thrown together, and
somehow resurrected. Freedom breaks chains.
A link connects a thousand neurons.

Stand silent in the background
and you're still no island. Vacant
atoms fill the room, from where
does the substance arise?

It's no matter; we cannot pass
through each other. Our bonds
are too strong, our strings too
tight.

The fuel in our flames still
flows freely. This ordinary
love is not what romance
promised to be; it's not
romance. Romance is a
dream, rudimentary love
is affection on the sidelines.

Each night I'm exasperated,
true fatigue born from
action. How many days

can I rest?

And yesterday's words
disappeared with the daylight.
This morning my muse
visited me, but I slept
through her insistence.

Now dead poems dot
the map, like pillaged
treasures. No one
can recover the now
invisible syllables.

Turn a cheek, turn
the page.

# New to Whom?

"The leaves are too green,
the sugar too white,
the water is too clear,
the soil too fertile.

"None of this will do
these are not foreign
tongues, but savage grunts,
animalistic moans.

"Quick! Load the ships!
Don't let them sense
your haste. Hide all the
precious stones you've
gathered. Truly we are
richer than the king!

"We went searching for
an adventure and stumbled
upon a dream. The royal
court won't believe us,
and perhaps it's better
that way; then this is ours!

"'Untouched paradise,' our

children will declare, and
who could deny them?

"In our humble expedition
seeking a new route,
a window to Heaven has
been opened to us.

"Providence has favored
us. For such unimaginable
bounty will our children
forever be indebted to
us!

"Come see what we've
found! Generations
will call us blessed,
and surely we are.

"Who can imagine
what lay beyond the
horizon? Truly this must
be how Adam felt in
the Garden.

"Who guides our steps
but the Divine! This gift
He's given us must never
be forgotten. Here we lay

our ebenezer, let no one
stand in our way."

# A Wolf and a Gavel

Why am I like this? Why
does your cardboard cutout
leave me in such distress? You
put a smile on and
mine fades. You lean into
a familiar feeling but I've
tasted it before, and it's
stale.
You're stale.

The inauthenticity kills
me. The imagined truth
cuts me deep. You whitewash
the chalkboard and I
still feel the dust on
your fingertips.

You try desperately to
powerwash any foreign
features from my face, but
I'm content in my sore
mind.

Please don't
try to change me, I'm

still learning to feel. I've
only recently begun to
peel the plastic from my
bones. The layers on my
face, they are the true
disgrace. The man
underneath it all, he is
who I'm looking for.

Please don't push me
on your train going
nowhere, and you can
take back your sheep's
clothing, it doesn't fit
anyway.

Maybe
if I could
lay down this gavel,
maybe
if I could
learn to love quietly,
maybe
then I could
speak frankly,
and leave this
vitriol behind me.

# Mundanity

Falling into routine feelings,
 falling like a worn out ceiling.
 Tattered, torn, and broken inside,
just hoping for a place to hide.

Can someone come pull
me out from the inside?
Hiding behind words,
hiding under feelings.

Tearing seams to make
stitches that won't break
me down, but filling in
spaces to avoid a small
frown.

There are toxins in my
blood and filters paint my
mouth. Why do I only
speak poison or potions?
Why is it all or nothing?

Am I a whisper or an
audible sound? Can
anyone hear me or

am I beginning to
drown? I'm lost in the
present but somehow
used to be found.

Is there freedom
in expression or
wisdom in words?

Am I worlds beyond
saving or chaff in
the wind? Please
don't burn the
fresh harvest, there
is fruit in the field.

My heart is tender,
my soul sewn
together in weeds;
there's a subtilty
in the breaths between
brokenness and the
battles I fight
for my life.

I'm a vapor quickly
fading, invisible but
free. I'm a Joshua
tree in the desert,

straining for food,
stretching toward
the sea.

# Holier

Holier, holier,
 how I wish that
 you could see.

Holier, holier,
 all the pain that
 you bring me.

I crash and burn
 while you're just
 holier than me.

I close my eyes
 and shut my mouth,
 try not to cry or
 let words spill out.

I sit and stare
 like a silent judge.
 You spit and share
 like a flightless dove.

Maybe it's because
 you're so much
 holier, holier,

holier than me.

You're holier, holier,
and only you can't
see.

Come down from
your high horse,
get out of that tree,
come down to the
living, come live
here with me.

There is life beyond
verses. Maybe life
is a stage, but
everyone can tell
you've rehearsed
this.

There's life in the
shadows, fertile
ground near the
cracked dirt. Please
don't let fear control
you.

You've covered your
fear, and nicknamed

it "love," you live with
a smile, but we all
see right through it.

Stop lying to yourself
and find the breadcrumbs
back to reality. You're still
worthy here. You can be
whole here. Please come
share bread with us. You
still belong here.

We'll wait at the door,
see you running from
the horizon. We'll
save a seat at the
table. Lay down
your expectations,
your prerequisites,
and all the silly
conditions you've
placed on your
love.

Love is a song here,
love sings, "you
belong here." You
don't have to pretend;
leave your mask,

don't hit "send."

You're a precious
flower in a gentle
hand, a sheep that
mistook that wolf
for a dog.

Come home, come
home. You don't
have to be holier,
holier,
any holier
than now.

# A backward glimpse with feet facing forward

Peering into pictures
of the past is a one-way
ticket to nostalgia.
You don't know how
strong is the homesickness
until you find yourself
suffocating beneath it.

Old friends, unrequited
loves, family members
forever frozen in time.
It's a broken time machine
that plays the same
song on repeat, a
bandage laced with
bacteria.

Leaving a foreign place
for a familiar bubble
can make you hungry
for expired meals. All
the faces you run into
become glimpses, shards,
or reflections of what

was so familiar yesterday.

Culture shock often
arrives upon the return;
"how great do we have
it!" or "how could I have
been so naïve?"

Short adventures away
from home keep the
grass greener and the
mind sharp. You must
burst your bubble to
recognize its size.

Venturing further can
help you join the present
if you can pull yourself
from the tempting lust
of the past.

Walk forward one step
at a time; it's okay to
peer briefly behind you
from time to time, but
growth is forward
without forgetting
lessons from the past.

One step, then
another; don't get
left behind.

# Same Old Story

Everyone has the same story,
the martyr with miraculously healed scars,
the rags to riches, streets to skyscrapers.

It's so inspiring
until
it's not.

We've romanticized the hero's journey,
we've glorified the rugged individual,
but at what cost?

When every narrative is a carbon copy
they all just lose their power.
When the unsung hero is stuck on repeat
no one wants to listen to the radio anymore.

Stop glorifying your simple stumbles,
quit magnifying your minute inconveniences;
you're devaluing narrative
and only promoting the need for further
evidence.

Just tell it like it is.
Everything doesn't

have to be political.
You don't have to
have a grandiose story.
It's okay to come from
mundanity, it's alright
to live in slight variations
of normal.

There are so many
shades of gray,
even different
degrees of purple.

Jumping to conclusions
just to be solid is
not admirable.
Please learn to live
in the nuance.

I'll meet you there,
the place where
the horizon meets
the sky, a place not
soaking wet, but
not completely dry.

I'll meet you
in the gray
where life

is lived
rather than
passing you
by.

# Gentle, Still Trembling

Shivering like on the movie screen,
 passing visions of lives I've never seen.
I've never been this close before,
I never thought I'd walk this shore.

My footprints checker the sand
but I don't know how this will end,
not that I'm looking for one.

Both of us shaking, uncertain, but solid.
How can this be something above
subconscious? It's only been dreams
before you uncovered my knitted seams.

A version of myself pulls the reigns
and the other pulls you closer.
A fractured soul, a fragile heart,
what happens if I'm torn apart?

Another month tangled in
your arms; are they weeds,
charms, or fertile soil? Are
you here for me or
here for you?

Every breath is precious, but
are they true? A faithful
friend, a missing clue.

I hold my heart out just
like you. I hold my heart
and catch my breath.

How will my heartbeat still?
And how are you still here?

# Target Audience

All these boxes, the pandering, the hollow
words,
  they all strike so swiftly to my core. It could be
  the Right, the Left, the pastor, the politician, the
  CEO. They force-feed me their doctrine, their
  views, their ways of being, and I gag at the
  thought.

  Please don't tell me how to live, don't
pigeonhole
  me, don't typecast me, don't you dare paint your
  words with glitter or gold for me; I know your
  soul is rust. I know you're a freshly groomed
lion,
  the whitewashed entrance to a coal mine.

  Your magic words won't enchant me, all your
  acting will never convince me; I can read
  through the filter you've placed between us.
  Your mask doesn't flatter me, your pressed
  and steamed shirts don't hide your wrinkles.

  I can see beyond the cardboard you cut out
  to deceive me. You've tried to pit me
  against what I know to be true, you thought

you could transfix me with your gaze,
your empty words. You thought I
would fight against myself.

But you're wrong. I've learned life is not
independence, I've learned to trust
others, not just myself. I've left
your myths far behind me.
Your screens don't
consume me. I'm
not a monkey,
nor a mirror;
I've grown.

All your plastic waste and
new smoky mirrors, they
will never slide past me.
My mind is on and open,
you don't get to control
me.

# She

Are these tests? Is this something to keep things
 fresh? How am I supposed to respond to this?
 What is the reason for all of this? For any of
this?

I'll stay on the line even if words aren't said.
I'll stay here but cannot be everywhere,
I cannot be everyone.

Are you trying to lead me to be the villain here?
Are you trying to push me away?
Do you want me to prove my love for you?

I don't think love should need proving, at least
not like this. Love is not ultimatums, nor is it
a series of tricks and tests.
Love is not a list of "dos" and "don'ts."

My love will never be a prescription, it won't be
a magic pill. There is no silver bullet that will
cure you of your ills. It's not a secret weapon
to bring an end to all ill will.

My love is a gentle whisper, a calm flame in the
dark and damp cold of night. It's a tattoo that

you can't remove. A hole in your favorite
sweater.
 It's the songbird at your window when you
haven't
 slept all night. It's words when you have none
and
 silence when you need it.

My love is not perfect, it's frayed, tattered, and
well-worn. It cannot be fished from the sea or
lost in a well. Sometimes it may be hard to
feel and sometimes it may not feel real,
but that doesn't mean that you're abandoned.

There is substance in this meal.

# such Superb intentions

Look at all the things you've done,
the medals you've won,
your shiny accomplishments, and
the people you've met.

What an achievement to have
arrived where you are today!
Your cardstocked buzzwords
and finely pressed suits.

How proud must you be of
who you've become! When's
the last time you spoke
with your younger self?

Would he even recognize
you? Surely it's not what
you know but who! Surely
you traded in your childhood
dreams for the right words
and a political savvy.

Smile wide, maybe then
you'll believe it, or at least
us. Paint peculiar progress

with diamond encrusted
pigment. Tell them all the
things you've done (or
taken credit for).

Look at all the new colors
painted over the old
guard's initiatives and
plans. So novel, so
innovative, so..
plastic.

Wow! New words to
hide old problems!
The status quo disguised
as progress. Minimal
growth celebrated
with all the fanfare.

Still..
I know a ripple is a ripple,
growth is growth. But,
we can see beyond your
bleached white teeth.
We feel you shake our
hands, can you feel any
life left inside us?

"Fight for me faithful

ones, I mean fight on
for your students! This
is my - no our - reputation
on the line.

"If you will not submit to
my Bureaucratic Oath
our growth will become
stagnate.

"I'm not here to fix this
system, I'm here to climb
one step closer to
influence, to power. I'm
here to further me, and
if your children grow
in the process, what
an added bonus!"

# Pure Propaganda

Why are there so many straight edges? So many
 sharp parts and pieces? The veil is so thin that
you
 hide behind. It's clear what you're hiding, so
clear that
 I wonder if you even notice it yourself.

 You're painting personalities and carrying as
many
 as you can on your back. "How many people
can we
 carry?" you never ask yourself, caught in some
hubris
 that you appear to be blind to.

Long ago you chose your side and
now you're just darkening the lines.
You're cutting the culture in pieces.
You're highlighting everywhere you
are and creating shadows around your
enemies; is that love?

I see through you and it's so hard not to
run in the opposite direction. Your "love"
is such poor acting, your values are so

political. When you try to feed me
your bread and wine, all I taste is
stale crackers and sweet grape juice.

What is your gospel? Who is your messiah?

We're so lost here and I even
hesitate to say that word because
I know it's your trigger. Please don't
hand me your map, you're not a cartographer.

Please do not come near me, I'm the
purple and gray that you fear. The more
you try to convince me, the less I draw near.
I'm not the villain here, but still

you are not either. I will not give
in to your fear called "love" just to
be another pawn in your scheme. I'm
not as far gone as you may try to convince
me. You're not the devil and I'm not the Savior.

Still,
the deceiver is among us, but the
the ratio is not what we've been told.
It's not one to one; the One we serve is
so much greater. I cannot give in to these
sweet smelling lies; there is so much more than

just two sides. We're factions from the same fractured
 whole.

Please do not continue to build your walls and
I will continue to construct these bridges.

I know the Body has many parts, but the
mouth cannot see what the eye beholds,
just as the eye may never taste the fruit
like the tongue. We are one, we are not
numbers to be won. I am your keeper and
you are mine.

# To New Beginnings

Not to gloat, but can I live
in this for a while? Don't want
to boast, but can I dance, can I smile?

Every day is Christmas
Eve, every day one less thing
to grieve. Can't keep it inside, you
know I can't hide.

I'm drinking from
the fire hose, but there's
more than one person holding
me steady, holding me
close.

Maybe this is what
true support looks
like. Maybe this is what
it is to be valued, to have more
than superficial gloves carrying
me.

This might be the perfect
combination, though I know
it's not perfect. Maybe this

is how the ordinary
becomes extraordinary.

Here's to a fresh start, a
whole heart, to finding
what I need and stumbling
into what I want along
the way.

# Go Beyond

I can fake it all
you want, but that won't
sustain any of us.
Flattery gets no one
anywhere.

Keep picking your
scabs and they
will never heal. Keep
lying to yourself and
you'll forget the
truth.

You can fill your
bucket with oil,
fat, or impotable
water, but none
of that will
satisfy you.

Your bucket
might as well
be pocked
with holes, for
nothing will

remain. You will
never have
enough, you will
forever be
unsatisfied,
unfulfilled.

Eternally scratch
the surface and
you'll never reach
the depths. You
may stumble upon
glimpses of
substance, but
nothing will truly
last. Nothing will
endure.

It's all temporal
if you let Fear
alone lead you.
Fear is an
influential leader,
but he will pull
you away from
all the potential
that Love has
for you. Fear is
the moon, but

Love is the sun;
are you satisfied
to follow a
reflection or will
you risk comfort
to follow the
true source?

When you step
beyond Fear or
even sidestep
him in favor of
Love, you'll find
unimaginable
images,
unfathomable
ideas, and
unprecedented
agency.

www.ingramcontent.com/pod-product-compliance
Lightning Source LLC
Chambersburg PA
CBHW061716130726
47996CB00006B/2351